How to Write
Your Physician Assistant
Personal Statement

Admissions directors and faculty share their expectations for
your PA school essay
and we teach you how to write it

Sue Edmondson
Duke Pasquini and Stephen Pasquini PA-C

The Physician Assistant Life
P.O. Box 250
McArthur, CA 96052
www.thepalife.com

Table of Contents

We dedicate this book to all the hard working PA school directors and faculty members who took time out of their busy schedules to work with us and grant us an interview. If it weren't for them this book would not be possible. And to you, our readers, for aspiring to make the world a better place one patient at a time.

The art of writing is discovering what you believe"

— Gustave Flaubert

Foreword

"I'm not looking to be entertained. I'm looking for a heartfelt, thoughtful explanation of why the PA profession is a good fit for you."

- Terry O'Donnell, Associate Professor and Chair of Physician Assistant Studies at Quinnipiac University.

The PA Life blog was started in 2013 as a way to connect PA applicants, students, and professionals with resources that make our lives as PAs better. When I was an applicant (over 12 years ago now), I couldn't find much on how to write a good personal statement.

I purchased a book about how to get into the PA school of your choice and followed the essay writing template.

As much as I loved the book, I can partially credit the section on essay writing for my initial failure to get an interview. Following a dry, cookie-cutter model of the personal statement seemed both safe and reasonable; it also proved unwise. I received four rejection letters.

In the blog, *How to Write the Perfect Physician Assistant School Application Essay*, I explained that I let go of this template (as well as my fear of failure), told my own story, and wrote an essay that really mattered. I know this because, despite my lower-than-required GPA, I applied to Rutgers and was asked to come for an interview just a few weeks later.

"We scoured the country to find PA administrators who were willing to share their secrets to writing a winning personal statement. This is the result of that search and the secret formula you have been seeking."

– Stephen Pasquini, PA-C

English and journalism were not my majors in college. My spelling is horrible, and I spent countless hours and days trying to force out a personal statement that would make the admissions committee happy.

The personal statement that got me an interview was written in less than an hour, sent to my dad to proofread, and mailed after his suggested edits.

The rest is history! I never thought much about this until later when my inbox started to fill with essays from prospective PA school applicants.

I never realized what a wide range of essays I would receive, or that I would spend the next two years, along with a passionate team of professional writers, in what would become The Physician Assistant Essay Collaborative.

This book is a culmination of the process of reading and working with hundreds of PA school applicants from across the country to help them find the right words to write an essay that matters.

We've gone one step further with this book by interviewing admissions directors and PA school faculty from across the country to pinpoint exactly what they want and don't want in a personal statement. This may be the single most important section of this book, and I encourage you to read it more than once.

I want to finish by saying that our team of editors are here for you, not only as a guide while you set out to write your personal statement, but also as a friend.

The journey for me has not always been an easy one. It has been a process of endless trial and error filled with self-doubt, occasional disappointment, some setbacks, and of course, successes. This is part of the process; it is important that you hang in there. If you ever feel discouraged, remember your ultimate purpose is to care for and love your patients. Let this be your guide as you write your personal statement and prepare to fulfill the long list of prerequisites for PA school.

Thank you so much for your support in purchasing this book. And if you've made it this far, I'd love for you to come say hi to me on my blog (thepalife.com) or Facebook page. I'll definitely respond and look forward to meeting you!

Cheers,

Stephen Pasquini, PA-C

The Expert Panel:

Twelve Top Ranking PA School Administrators Explain What They Want in Your Personal Statement

TIRED OF THE GUESSING GAME?

You've finally finished your personal statement and it's perfect.

There's not a grammar or spelling error in sight. Your mother, best friend, and barista at the local coffee bar all think it's a winner.

The character count is right. There's just one thing to consider before hitting the "send" button — will it meet the admission team's expectations?

How will you know? CASPA guidelines are vague — "Write a brief statement expressing your motivation or desire to become a physician assistant." School websites aren't generally more helpful.

Do they want to hear that you've dreamed of becoming a PA since you were five and loved your toy stethoscope? Are they interested in your volunteer work at a homeless shelter? Will it help that you've been a science nerd since 9th grade biology? How should you tell your story? Should it read like a textbook, a novel, or something in between?

The fact is there hasn't been much guidance.

UNTIL NOW!

Admissions directors and faculty from PA programs across the country have shared their thoughts on personal statements — what they hope to see, what they wish they'd never see, and tips to make an essay shine. Each school has a unique perspective, but common themes arise.

First things first

Before writing one word, think about your audience. Ask yourself the following questions: Are you applying to several programs or are you targeting a specific school, like Wake Forest University, which focuses on building future leaders in the PA profession or Emory, that values clinical experience and community service? Does your preferred program use clinical, hands-on training like Georgia Regents University?

"I encourage applicants to research programs in depth. Go to open houses if possible," says Janie McDaniel, BSMT, Assistant Professor, Wake Forest School of Medicine. "A lot of programs look at non-cognitive matters or take a holistic approach, using a rubric of GPAs, GRE scores, patient care hours, and personal statements. Others have a minimum GPA requirement. Know what the program is hoping for in an applicant."

If applying to a specific program, highlight your experiences, training, skills, and traits that relate to the school's preferences.

"Clinical experience and community service are very important to us. We love for applicants to describe what they've done clinically. Take a patient or two and tell us about them, says Allan Platt, PA-C, MMSc,

Director of Admissions, Emory Physician Assistant Program. "We also want to know about your involvement in community service even if it's not medically related. Have you gone on a mission? Worked with a homeless population? Tell us how those experiences impacted you."

If your targeted program uses CASPA, or if you're applying to a number of schools, no worries. "A well-written essay will speak to all programs," says Darwin Brown, MPH, PA-C, Associate Program Director and Director of Clinical Education at UNMC.

It was a dark and stormy night in the back of the ambulance

Universally, interviewees mentioned the use of drama in essays, and not in a positive way.

"A lot of people start with a dramatic paragraph. I personally find that too scripted. I'm not looking to be entertained. I'm looking for a heartfelt, thoughtful explanation of why the PA profession is a good fit for you," says Terry O'Donnell, BS, MAT, MHS, Associate Professor and Chair of Physician Assistant Studies at Quinnipiac University.

"Over the top drama doesn't wow. It does the opposite," says Audra Perrino, MS, Director of Admissions at Stony Brook University Physician Assistant Program.

"Go for the heart, not the drama," says Lori Palfreyman, MS, PA-C, Faculty Chair of the Admissions Committee at Rutgers University PA Program.

"Our faculty has different opinions on story telling aspects, but everyone agrees — if your personal statement is superficial, then you have a problem," says Grace Landel, MEd, PA-C, Program Director□Joint MSPAS/MPH Program, Touro University California.

When I was 10 I had my tonsils removed

The whole point of the personal statement is to educate admissions personnel about the subjective factors that grades and test scores can't reveal. Everyone wants to know the journey that brought you to this point, with a caveat. No one wants to hear about that stethoscope you played with as a five-year old or how you spoon-fed your sick grandmother (as heartwarming a story as it is).

Tim Quigley, MPH, PA-C, Director of Student Affairs at MEDEX NW Division of Physician Assistant Studies, explains. "We'd rather hear about your work with patients than about a family member's illness. Not to say it's unimportant, but we expect you've gone on from that and done other things. Talking about more recent events shows a certain level of maturity and experience. Avoid first person family stories and focus on real patients."

"It's common for applicants to start the essay with a childhood experience. It can be a starting point, but move on quickly," says Judith Stallings, EdD, MHE, PA-C, Associate Director of Admissions at Georgia Regents University.

"It's not impressive when someone writes paragraphs about personal experiences — they shouldn't be the overriding theme of the essay. If a family member was sick and that was your first care-giving experience, mention it in a sentence or two. The day-in and day-out details are unnecessary," Palfreyman says.

"Some students talk too much about their personal stories and not enough about their professional experiences. The essay should be about experiences with patients," says Leah P. Baldwin, Associate Director of Graduate and Professional Programs Admissions, Pacific University.

"What we're looking for is a passion for the profession and patients. Sometimes when the word 'I' appears frequently in a statement, it tells me the applicant is not as concerned about the profession as he is himself," O'Donnell says.

"If every sentence starts with 'I,' you're missing the opportunity to tell us what we get out of accepting you into our program," Palfreyman adds.

I have a passion to serve

Platitudes waste space. You wouldn't be applying to PA school if you didn't have a passion/calling/desire for the profession. Generalizations don't help admissions personnel discover the factors that set you apart from someone else with similar grades, scores and experience.

"One of the first things we look for is their motivation to be a PA. We want an essay that's personal, not generic. Don't give us the definition of a PA or quote from our website," Quigley says. "The writer needs to remember we get 1,000 applications, so the essay needs to be unique enough to catch an eye. It's important to highlight why your experiences would make you a great PA."

"My perspective is that this is the opportunity for applicants to show us who they really are," Brown says. "We want to know who you are and how you got here. Often those with healthcare experience offer too little insight into what they've gained from their work. We want to know why those experiences are important."

"Common platitudes like, 'I want to help people,' aren't useful. We want people who can communicate with patients, so write about those experiences. We use the essay to see what's unique about this individual and how they got to this point. What's their journey? Why have you chosen to be a PA? How did you confirm your interest and why is it important to you?" says Wayne Stuart, MD, Director, DeSales University Physician Assistant Program.

"The essay needs to be about the applicant. When three-quarters of an essay describes a PA's job, we don't learn anything about the applicant," Landel says. "Instead focus on what you've done that has led you to seek out the PA profession. Key in on the experiences that brought you to the fork in the road and tell us why you took the path to become a PA."

"Applicants need to tell a real story about how they got to the point of applying, based upon numerous events that led to this career choice. Come up with a list of personality traits needed in healthcare work — empathy, a desire to help others," Perrino says. "Tie events in your life to developing the attributes and traits that will make you a good PA. One sentence is often enough. For example, 'I was an athlete and learned to work with a team.' We like to hear about the individualized journey. You need to show me who you are and what you have to contribute. It can be as simple as developing the list of your traits into sentences."

"This is the opportunity to express how you connect with patients on a human level. It's the subjective part of the application — the part that grades and work history don't explain," Palfreyman says. "If one of your reasons for wanting to be a PA is connecting with patients on a deeper level, show what you've learned or describe your traits that will help you fill that role."

"You should include something about your personal strengths to show that you are highly organized or a hard worker," Stallings says.

"The essay should show some level of maturity and understanding about the physician-led PA team. Why does the profession apply to this applicant? Most applicants will have worked with a PA. Those experiences are the ones to write about," says Dennis Brown, PA-C, MPH, Clinical Assistant Professor of Physician Assistant Studies, Director of Physician Assistant Program at Quinnipiac University.

"We use the essay to discover what is unique about this individual and how he got to this point. What is their journey? My perspective is that this is the opportunity for applicants to show us who they really are," Darwin Brown says.

If you're invited to write a supplemental essay, DO NOT simply cut and paste your CASPA personal statement.

"That won't impress us," Platt says.

What? You could have been a doctor!

It should be a no-brainer. But it's omitted often enough for interviewees to mention it — they need to know why you've targeted this profession and not another healthcare related job.

"Why have you chosen PA school and not medical or nursing school? What happened in your journey to bring you to this decision? If you want me to understand how you reached this point in your life, tell me about your motivations," Perrino says.

"If someone talks about passion for the profession in the essay, but they haven't done much, there's a real disconnect. The strongest essays are where I really get a feeling for why a person has chosen this profession in a non-text book like description," O'Donnell says.

So you volunteered at a food pantry

"If you volunteered, tell us what about that experience impacted you. It doesn't have to be a healthcare related situation," Palfreyman says. "If helping at a women's shelter changed you in a way that will make you a better PA, talk about it."

"You don't need to leave the country for a mission for volunteer work to matter," Baldwin says.

"Tell us about community service, especially as it relates to our mission of serving diverse and underserved populations," Quigley says.

"If your community service work provided the drive for you to apply, tell us about it," Dennis Brown says.

"If you worked with underserved populations, tell how that impacted your perception of health care," McDaniel says.

It's not only what you want

"I'll want to know what you can contribute to our program and your future patients," Perrino says.

"What do we gain as a program? What personal traits do you have that will benefit patients?" Palfreyman says. "Think about what we want for the end product — passionate, empathetic, smart PAs. What personal skills do you have that meet that criteria?"

"Applicants should describe why they fit into our program. We're known for our clinical, hands-on training," Stallings says. "Applicants should say that's what they're looking for and describe the skills they already have in that area."

"Have you researched us? Go beyond the website to find out about our program," Platt says.

I bombed my junior year and other anomalies

The personal statement offers a unique opportunity to explain why you've had bumps in the road. Everyone wants to hear the explanation, but not in too much detail. Interviewees wanted to know what led to the problem — perhaps the death of a parent — not about childhood incidents such as abuse or neglect.

"If there are weaknesses in your application, don't assume anyone will know why. If you haven't done volunteer work maybe it's because you're economically disadvantaged and need to work full-time," Palfreyman says.

"Use part of the essay to explain that. If you have a dip in grades, explain what happened in a brief sentence or two — you have to balance between being too personal and not personal enough. We look for people who are mature enough to take ownership of their weaknesses."

"If there are irregularities, say you didn't do well in school, you should address it. We have to draw the line somewhere, and the personal statement is one opportunity to explain. That may be your only opportunity — the information may not be requested in a supplemental essay," Landel says.

Quigley agrees. "Address academic difficulties. Explain what was happening at the time. We look for a trajectory of academic improvement and clinical experience that shows increasing responsibilities."

"If we have applicants who have been out of school for a while — maybe they're in their late 20's or early 30's — we want to know what they've been doing. They need to talk about work experience to give us a sense of how much time they've spent in healthcare related fields and what they've gained as a result," Stallings says.

This isn't your first rodeo

"If you're reapplying, it's important to explain what's different this time. Don't hand in the same application. I love it when applicants say, 'These are the things I did to strengthen my skills.' It shows maturity and ownership," Palfreyman says.

"If you've applied the year before, don't copy the same information for the new application. You should update it by detailing your recent experiences. Have you completed more PA shadowing hours? Increased your work experience? Improved your GPA? The essay is the first place we find out about it," Stallings says.

Getting from A to Z

Structure is very important to your essay, interviewees say. It's easiest to follow a story written in chronological order, but it's not mandatory. Just make sure you cover all your relevant experiences and link them by time you reach the conclusion.

"Make sure the essay is as concise as possible with no gaps in time," Stallings says.

"We're just trying to find out your life's journey. We want to know who you are and how you got here. Try to tell it in a coherent way," Platt says.

"Connect the dots," Palfreyman says.

"An excellent personal statement doesn't sound rehearsed. It's all about structure, like chapters in a book," Perrino says.

Your personal statement must tell a story — your story. Skip the sirens and flashing lights. Instead, frame the story with experiences that focus on development of your skills and explain your desire to be a PA.

"You do need some catch or hook to keep us reading," Landel says.

HOOK

Darwin Brown explains the benefit of a hook in more detail. "Use a hook, but don't spend too much time on it. The hook is the skeleton to hang the material on. If you have a passion for running, link that dedication to your work ethic."

"Don't spend three quarters of the essay on one experience. We rather learn about everything you've done — shadowing, volunteer work, class work — things you have control over," Baldwin says.

An invitation to the interview is the bottom line.

"If after reading an essay the committee members want to meet the applicant, it's been done well," Palfreyman says.

Writing is rewriting

You might not want to hear it, but it's true. Sure, you've gone over and over your essay, but that's not enough. Every interviewee recommends having several others read it for grammar and spelling errors as well as structure and cohesion.

Whether you use friends, family, or professional editors, make sure the essay is yours. "The personal statement should be polished, but be written by you. Sometimes we have people write a statement during the interview. If the personal statement doesn't conform to what is written during the interview, it can be a problem," Stuart says.

Little things are big

Yes, you've checked your essay for errors, but check it again. Spelling and grammar errors are unacceptable.

"It's a reflection of your capabilities and education," McDaniel says.

"There is no excuse for errors in spelling and grammar," Palfreyman says.

"Those errors are immediate red flags," Stuart says.

"The essay is the first opportunity to show some degree of potential for the program and that you have the basic skills to write in an appropriate fashion," Darwin Brown says. "The ability to communicate is an important skillset for all healthcare professionals. If you can't spell, it's dangerous."

While some interviewees said one error wouldn't prevent an invitation to interview, there's no reason to take that chance. And whatever you do, get the title of the profession right.

"If you write 'physician's assistant,' it triggers concern. It tells us you don't really understand what the profession is about," Baldwin says.

Last but not least, read the rules.

"Be sure to follow instructions. The first question on our applicant self-assessment form is, 'Have you followed the instructions?' It's amazing how many people don't," Landel says.

The bottom line

Don't underestimate the value of the personal statement. It's your opportunity to stand out from the crowd of the (literally) thousand other people applying for the same slot.

CHAPTER 2

Writing Your Personal Statement

"This is how you do it: you sit down at the keyboard and you put one word after another until it's done. It's that easy, and that hard."

– Neil Gaiman

Now that you know what admissions directors look for in application essays, how will you write one that sets you apart from the crowd?

We will take you step-by-step through the process of writing your essay.

Here you'll learn everything you need to know about writing an effective personal statement, with tips and real-world examples.

A "personal statement" is different from an essay in that it is not simply a statement of facts and figures, but a form of writing that combines telling a story (your story) and selling a product (you) to a reader who is selecting a few from thousands of potential applicants.

Some of what we will discuss may seem obvious. In fact, it is. You probably learned much of this in grade school. If it weren't for the subtleties that you'll learn here, all the essays we receive would be ready to ship.

The truth is, no matter how well-intentioned or qualified you may be, the art of selling yourself, differentiating yourself, explaining yourself, and telling your life story in the CASPA required 5,000 characters or less is extremely difficult.

Form

It's simple, every essay must have these three parts:

1. An introduction – tell the reader what you're going to tell them.

2. A body – tell them

3. A conclusion – tell them what you told them.

It sounds simple, possibly even dull. It can be, but when you combine this basic outline with good prose and images the reader can visualize in their head, you'll have a quality essay

---

The Introduction

"The scariest moment is always just before you start."

- Stephen King, On Writing

You have just a few seconds to seize the attention of a new reader. Get it right, and you may well be on your way to an interview. Get it wrong and your essay will end up in the pile with thousands of others labeled "forgettable."

So what makes a great introduction?

One method is to us an anecdote. An anecdote creates an image in the reader's mind. You know the old saying, "A picture is worth a thousand words." The image you create in your essay is worth a thousand words.

Here's an example:

When I was a freshman in college, I visited my history TA to see why I was earning a C. He grabbed my essay test from his desk, paged through it, smiled, and said, "Your problem is you don't organize your thoughts. It's like you have a bunch of wheels flying around in your head. You put them on paper the same way. They're just all wheels scattered about in your essay. You don't clarify the steering wheel from the front wheels, the back wheels, the right wheels, the left wheels, and so on."

He created an image in my mind just like I'm sure it does in yours. I was frustrated.

"What should I do?"

"Take a writing class," he answered.

And that's what I did. (By the way, never start a sentence with a conjunction in your essay).

My expository writing teacher told our class about the same three parts of an essay that I listed in the opening. At the time, it went right over my head. I didn't understand what the teacher was saying until a couple weeks before class ended. I ended up getting a D in the class.

I took my D and my new knowledge into the real world where I earned my Master's Degree, published three books, wrote several articles that were published in national magazines, and taught speech and writing to high school students.

Maybe you've had a similar experience — bombed a chemistry class, only to receive an A when you took it again. Perhaps you cared for a patient who taught you the importance of empathy, human touch, and being a good listener.

The anecdote sets the theme of your essay, and prepares the reader for what comes next.

The following are examples of introductions by our clients that received interviews and were later accepted into PA school.

Introduction Example 1

> *In a world where quixotic ideals of our youth are quickly dismissed as meaningless clichés, it is easy for our heart's true passion to drown in a sea of disingenuous ambitions. Oftentimes, it takes many trials and failures as well as achievements, for one to truly find himself. I purposelessly moved through the motions of life. All my previous goals felt forced and insincere until I began to consider becoming a physician assistant. Switching majors or choosing career paths based on their financial prospects or practicality didn't bring me happiness. My personal life and relationships suffered; I became disheartened with school and felt unfulfilled.*

What makes this a good introduction?

1. My first reaction was that this was over the top until I read further. This "quixotic" introduction makes the reader think of Don Quixote fighting windmills and trying to achieve unrealistic ideals. Don Quixote may have been an old man, but this author ties the quixotic dreams to the unrealistic ideals of his youth. It immediately gets the reader wondering what's next. It also makes the reader believe this applicant is a thinker.

2. The author creates the image of the "heart's true passion" drowning in disingenuous ambitions. You picture the ideals slowing sinking like the Titanic.

3. Then the author mentions trials and failures as a way of finding who he is.

4. The beauty of all this is that the author then mentions that everything seemed forced or worthless (even though he didn't use the term worthless) until he considered becoming a PA.

5. A lot is covered in this one paragraph.

6. The author realized that it wasn't money that would bring him happiness, but something else.

7. This paragraph separates this applicant from 95% of the other applicants.

Introduction Example 2

I was only an observer, wearing a blue cotton blouse with the word, "VOLUNTEER," written across my chest when the paramedic swiftly maneuvered the stretcher into the trauma bay. The paramedic looked concerned but spoke with confidence, 'This is an eighteen-year-old female who was in a car accident. She overdosed while driving and ran straight into a light pole.'

What makes this a good introduction?

1. We have a picture of her standing there with the word "VOLUNTEER" written across her chest. We immediately know she is volunteering and observing.

2. You can picture her standing there as the stretcher is rolled (maneuvered) into the trauma bay where we now know she's doing her observing.

3. She observes both the concern and confidence of the paramedic.

4. We know the woman was in a car accident, had overdosed, and hit a light pole.

5. The introduction is short.

6. It makes the reader want to know what happens next and how it affects her.

Other Types of Introductions

The way you choose to write your introduction will depend on the type of essay you write and how you plan to engage your reader. Above we discussed one of the most common and effective tactics, using an anecdote. There are certainly other ways to engage the reader and make him/her want to keep reading.

Let's take a look at three other common types of introductions you could effectively use:

1. Open with a Quote

   Introducing your essay with a quote can establish your viewpoint on the topic and help create a solid foundation on which to begin your essay.

   Here is an example:

"Whatever your heart desires, I desire for you." This note was printed on the inside of a Valentine's Day card I received from an elderly patient during my second year as a CNA…

2. Ask a Question

The introduction may have one or more questions posed to the reader. When you pose a question in your introduction, you will need to address the answer throughout your essay. For example you could ask, "How do you get back on your feet after a difficult life event?" With this question in mind, the main part of your essay might address this difficult life event and how you over-came it.

Here is an example:

I had just failed my freshman year of college, flunking every course except for my philosophy class because of a philosophy professor who never failed anyone. What happened? How did I get here?

3. Give an Overview

Your goal is to provide the reader with enough information that he or she can focus on the points you present in the body of your essay.

Here is an example:

Many experiences led me to the decision to become a physician assistant, but three experiences stand out above the rest: Shirley, a patient I met while working as an EMT, an open heart surgery that lasted ten hours, and the summer I shadowed a PA…

The Body

> "The difference between the right word and the almost right word is the difference between lightning and a lightning bug."
>
> - Mark Twain

The body of your essay is the glue that holds your personal statement together. It is also the darkest part of the forest. In other words, it is where most people get incredibly lost. If you wander off, you will lose your readers down a long and winding path from which they may never return.

Do this right, and at the end of the trail there will be a sign pointing to your PA school interview. Do this wrong, and you can turn around and take the long trail back to the parking lot.

Once you have your reader's attention with your unforgettable introduction, you need to keep it.

What should you include in your body?

Reflect back to section one and what the admissions directors said:

- Start with your introduction. Where are you leading us?

- Then, as our interviewees suggested, "You need to tell a story – your story, a real story about how you got to the point of applying, based upon numerous events that led to this career choice."

- "Tell it in a coherent way." "Connect the dots." "It's all about structure, like chapters in a book."

- "Skip the sirens and flashing lights. Instead, frame your story with experiences that focus on development of your skills and explain your desire to be a PA."

What makes you special? A lot of people have good grades, many hours of experience, and a desire to help people. Why do you stand out from the rest? Use the body of your essay to answer the all-important questions:

1. Why do you want to be a PA?
2. What have you done that makes you unique
   a. volunteer activities
   b. work experience
   c. shadowing hours
3. Address any shortcomings you may have.

Below are two samples from applicants who received interviews.

Body Example 1

The second thing that influenced my decision to become a PA took place when I was given the opportunity to observe an aortic valve replacement. My fascination from the first buzz of the saw to suturing the chest never wavered through ten hours and two surgeries. During the coronary bypass graft in the second surgery, a nurse casually mentioned, "That's a PA harvesting the vein."

Before that, I did not realize PAs could specialize in many areas of medicine. This appealed to me, so I began exploring a career as a physician assistant. That summer I shadowed Sean, a General Surgery PA, who was responsible for supervising PA students while they were doing their clinical rotations. I kept a list of every type of surgery I saw, and often went home with a list of new diseases to research. Sean's PA students were physiology lovers like me. They

> *loved learning new things and applying their knowledge. Their enthusiasm was unmatched by anyone I had met in any other clinical setting. Learning alongside them cemented my desire to become a PA.*

What works about this portion of the body of this essay?

1. We know it is part of a list of at least two reasons this applicant decided to become a PA.

2. She was given the opportunity to observe an aortic valve replacement surgery. (great opportunity)

3. The author talks about her fascination from the first buzz of the saw to the suturing. (We get the feeling she is in her element and feels comfortable there.)

4. She was there for ten hours and two surgeries. That shows dedication and patience. Yet, she doesn't once tell us she's dedicated or patient.

5. She introduces us to the fact that it is a PA who harvests the vein. This impresses her and creates a desire to look into the PA profession.

6. The author lets us know how she realized PAs can specialize.

7. Her interests lead her to shadow a PA.

8. She keeps a list of every type of surgery she saw. Again, without telling us, we know she's dedicated and hardworking. Her actions tell us that she is. "Actions speak louder than words."

9. Instead of saying, "I am a physiology lover," she says, "Sean's PA students were physiology lovers like me. They loved learning new things and applying their knowledge." She moves the action to the group of which she is a part so the focus isn't just on her.

10. She goes on to say, "Their enthusiasm was unmatched by anyone I had met..."

11. She now cleverly says, "Learning alongside them cemented my desire to become a PA." Again she uses the group to emphasis her strengths.

Body Example 2

Two incidents further led me to the decision to become a PA. Nancy had undergone hip-replacement surgery and was in severe pain during recovery. She was immobile and suffering from the onset of dementia. The nursing assistant and I were responsible for changing her incontinence pad. She moaned, "How could you do this to me? How dare you?" We attempted to elevate Nancy's hips while I tried to mitigate Nancy's pain. The nursing assistant continued while I held Nancy's hand. She squeezed my hand with each movement as if she were attempting to transfer the pain to me. She winced, but her yelling stopped. While short-lasting, our intertwined fingers created an enduring, tangible symbol of care. Until that moment, I had not realized the powerful impact human touch can create. I use my hands every day to listen to respirations and pulses, conduct pulmonary function tests, and administer allergy shots. Because of Nancy, I always take the initiative to make a human connection, whether a touch on the shoulder or pat on the back.

Then came Alex, a timid, young boy of about four years old who was afflicted by atopic dermatitis. He entered into my care while I was working as a patient care tech at an allergy and asthma clinic. Alex was crying, scratching the bleeding rash covering his legs, and refusing to let me take his vitals. I quickly gathered a Band-Aid, ointment, and a Captain America sticker before wiping off his bloody leg and applying ointment to the rash. He stopped crying.

After applying the bandage, I said, "If I can listen to your heart, you can have this Captain America sticker." He complied reluctantly, but I completed the assessment and gave him the sticker. Alex slapped the sticker on his chest and smiled with pride as I guided him and his mother to their room.

Nothing symbolizes compassion more than the human hand, with its power to create a physical and emotional connection from one being to another. Becoming a PA would offer many opportunities to experience the emotional bond of human touch like what I shared with Nancy and Alex.

What works about this portion of the body of this essay?

1. We immediately know there are two incidents that influenced her to become a PA.

2. She introduces us to Nancy who we know has dementia and had her hip replaced.

3. We have a picture of the writer holding Nancy's hand while Nancy is screaming. Nancy squeezes the writer's hand.

4. The writer uses the hand as a symbol of the relationship with the patient. She says that it's like Nancy is trying to pass her pain to her. (This is insightful)

5. She ties it all together with these words, "Until that moment, I had not realized the powerful impact human touch can create. I

use my hands every day to listen to respirations and pulses, conduct pulmonary function tests, and administer allergy shots. Because of Nancy, I always take the initiative to make a human connection, whether a touch on the shoulder or pat on the back."

6. She then introduces us to the second incident that influenced her to become a PA. She tells us about four-year old Alex.

7. She explains why he's there and how he scratches himself. She also tells us why she is there working with him.

8. We have an image of her grabbing a Band-Aid, ointment, and a Captain America sticker. We know it makes him stop crying.

9. She offers him an incentive of the Captain America sticker if he will let her listen to his heart. He complies. We can picture it all. We see him slap the sticker on his chest and smile with pride as the writer guides him to his mom.

10. Finally, the writer ties it all together by saying, "Nothing symbolizes compassion more than the human hand, with its power to create a physical and emotional connection from one being to another. Becoming a PA would offer many opportunities to experience the emotional bond of human touch like what I shared with Nancy and Alex."

Seven Rules to Follow While Writing the Body of Your Essay

Below are five rules you should always follow when constructing the body of your PA school personal statement. Review each rule carefully before and after you write your personal statement.

Rule 1: Show – Don't Tell

You'll do this by creating images the readers will not forget.

Presenters at writers' conferences repeatedly tell authors to show and not tell. The difficulty comes from thinking of showing and telling as two completely different ways of writing, when, in fact, showing and telling overlap like two interlocking rings.

You need to tell the reader your story. The difference is that in telling your story you create an image in the reader's mind by using the five senses (showing). Think of telling as giving the reader a list of facts and generalizations. No image is created in their mind.

Think of the anecdote about the wheels used earlier. You can visualize the TA grabbing the essay, smiling at the student, and talking about the wheels. You can picture all those wheels scattered about in some random order. The story and the image convey his message about the importance of organization.

EXAMPLE 1: Telling Versus Showing.

Telling: The doctor closed the wound.

Showing: Blood covered the doctor's surgical gloves as he stapled the two-inch wound in Tom's thigh.

EXAMPLE 2: Show and Tell Using the Five Senses

That previous example is a simple one. Let's look at a longer more complicated example.

Think back on the "show and tell" you did when you were in elementary school. Children would bring one of their favorite toys and tell the class about it. In this example, it's a teddy bear. The teddy bear is the image the child holds up for the class to see. It's concrete. How clear would the image be if the child left the teddy bear at home and only talked about it? *Not very clear.* (By the way, don't use fragments in your essay,)

You don't want to figuratively leave your teddy bear home and merely tell us about it in your essay. You don't have the option of bringing your teddy bear (your experience or passion) so you need to make the reader see them by creating a picture in the reader's mind.

The child in the show and tell example holds the bear in his/her hands for everyone to see and then hands it to the boy in the first row. The children pass it around the room. Each child looks at it, squeezes it, smells it, and pulls the loop on its back. One boy can't resist taking a lick of Teddy's fur. "Yuck! It tastes like soap," he says. Each student learns that Teddy smells like fabric softener, feels soft and cuddly like a pillow with fur. One unfortunate child learns it tastes like soap. The children see the fur is a mixture of dark and light browns, and figure out that it talks when you pull the loop on his back. The bear says, "Hello, my name is Teddy."

You know how Teddy smells, feels, looks, tastes, and sounds because the example includes the five senses. You need to do this as you write about your passion and experience. You don't have to bring four or five teddy bears to your essay. One or two is enough.

Always remember is it much better to give an example that shows you are compassionate, dependable, and caring than to tell the reader you are compassionate, dependable, and caring.

Rule 2: Avoid Using Passive Voice.

You want your readers to visualize you as a confident experienced applicant. Be direct. Go straight to the point. Don't beat around the bush.

EXAMPLE #1: Passive Voice Versus Active Voice

Let's start off with a very simple example.

Active: Bill hit the ball.

Passive: The ball was hit by Bill.

Active: Bill hit the ball over the fence at Veterans' Field.

Passive: While at Veterans' Field, the ball was hit by Bill over the fence.

Notice how much more direct active voice is over passive voice.

EXAMPLE #2: Passive Voice Versus Active Voice

Active: Dr. Brown closed the wound.

Passive: The wound was closed by Dr. Brown.

Active: St. Joseph's Hospital provided me with many valuable medical experiences.

Passive: I received a lot of valuable medical experiences at St. Joseph's Hospital.

Passive: When I worked at St. Joseph's Hospital, I received a lot of valuable medical experience.

Note: Use action verbs whenever possible. They propel the story forward and imply confidence.

Rule 3: Keep Sentences Short

Why? They're a lot easier to read.

EXAMPLE:

Original Sentence: As an AmeriCorps volunteer, I had many responsibilities that included providing medical aid, helping the local doctor, who asked me to work with him, visiting homes in the poor community, and providing literacy help, along with a regular weekend schedule, where I worked at the library by reading to four and five-year olds.

Improved Sentence(s): AmeriCorps provided me with many valuable experiences. They included providing medical aid, helping the local doctor, teaching adult literacy classes, and reading to four and five-year-olds on the weekends.

Same information, easier to read. Notice how it also eliminates the use of "I," a word often red-flagged by Admissions personnel.

If you need help with constructing short sentences, outline your paragraph. Most of us were taught to start a paragraph with a topic sentence, and then provide at least three supporting points.

Here's the above example in outline form. This is deductive reasoning. Your paragraph goes from the general to the specific.

AmeriCorps provided me with many valuable experiences.

a) Helped the local doctor
b) Provided medical aid
c) Taught adult literacy classes
d) Read stories to four and five-year olds

The example below is inductive reasoning. You move from the specific to the general.

A) Helped the local doctor
B) Provided medical aid
C) Taught adult literacy classes
D) Read stories to four and five-year olds

AmeriCorps provided me with many valuable experiences.

Consider writing this kind of outline for each paragraph. Sometimes use deductive reasoning and another time use inductive reasoning. Create a topic sentence for each of the topics you want to discuss in your essay. (It can go at the beginning or the end.) Once done, go back and write at least three supporting points.

Keep in mind, these are guidelines. Nothing is black and white. There may be a place for passive voice, or a need to tell rather than show. You could use inductive reasoning instead of deductive reasoning by placing the topic sentence at the end instead of the beginning.

Rule 4: Get Rid of Unnecessary Words

`"The most valuable of all talents is that of never using two words when one will do"

– Thomas Jefferson

Too many words have the same effect as long sentences. They distract the reader and make your images fuzzy.

Think of the show and tell example with the teddy bear. When you get too wordy, it's like putting a piece of semi-clear plastic between you and your audience. They can see you and the teddy bear, but not very clearly.

Note: Too many short sentences can be as bad as too many long sentences. Vary them. If your essay sounds choppy, then combine sentences by adding a conjunction or use some other method to make the essay flow better. (It's best to do this one paragraph at a time.)

Rule 5: Make Every Paragraph Relevant, Detailed, and Purposefully Connected

How do you determine relevance? It's easier than you think. Ask the question, "Will this paragraph make the admissions committee want to invite me to an interview?" That determines relevance. Be sure you provide specific details, and make sure everything is purposefully connected.

It's only after you have what you hope is a completed essay that you can make this decision.

Note: The essay readers will most likely have a rubric to follow when reading your essay. They will score your paragraphs or your entire essay using point values from 0 to 4 with four being the best. Here's a sample rubric. Keep this rubric in mind when writing your essay:

4 relevant, detailed, and purposefully connected
3 appropriate, clear, and connected
2 minimal, vague, cursory
1 little or nothing
0 Nothing

Rule 6: Use First Names Whenever Possible

If you are writing about a patient or a PA, and you find yourself repeatedly saying the patient or the PA, give them a first name and then alternate between using their name and the pronouns him, her, she, and he. Make up a name and never use a last name. This is not a HIPPA violation.

Rule 7: Spell PAs and Physician Assistant Correctly

Physician assistant is written **physician assistant** not physician's assistant and it is not capitalized unless it begins a sentence like this one or in a title like Rule 7.

The plural of PA is written PAs. The possessive would be PA's. (e.g. The PA's schedule was filled.)

Concluding Your Essay

"I've learned that people will forget what you said, people will forget what you did, but people will never forget how you made them feel."

–Maya Angelou

Have you ever caught yourself at the end of a wonderful book, fighting away tears, and lamenting the fact you had reached the final sentence? If so, then you have witnessed masterful writing along with an effective conclusion. As the quote above points out, people will forget facts, possibly even deeds, but they will never forget how you made them feel.

Your conclusion is the place to highlight the points made in your essay in a short paragraph. The conclusion of your essay is like the last kiss at the end of a first date. It should always leave the recipient wanting more.

You might do one of the following:

1. Conclude by linking the last paragraph to the first, perhaps by repeating a word or phrase you used at the beginning.

2. Tell them what you told them." Make it brief, make it simple, and make it remarkable.

Examples of Effective Personal Statement Conclusions

EXAMPLE #1

We never know whether our patient will be a drug dealer, alcohol abuser, a mother, father, son, or daughter. The one thing I know is that they must all be treated with respect and given the treatment they deserve. We laugh and smile when we succeed or find a man with his finger stuck in a drain. We cry when we fail or our patient dies. Mistakes and failures are a reality faced by PAs, doctors, and

EMTs every time they encounter a patient, but only those who do not fear failure can succeed. They are the ones who look forward to going to work every day with the chance to make a positive difference. These are my beliefs. These are the reasons I want to be a PA.

This is a good conclusion for the following reasons:

1. This applicant started her essay discussing a drug dealer they picked up on her first shift as an EMT. She also mentioned that when they save a person's life, it can easily be the life of a "mother, father, son, or daughter." This makes it stronger and more inclusive.

2. The essay mentions how her friends thought her work with Alzheimer's patients was meaningless. So she now mentions that every patient should be respected.

3. The applicant reminds the reader that she understands from her own experience that there will be successes and failures, and mentions the odd incident about a man who got his finger caught in a drain to illustrate something unusual.

4. The writer makes the point that even though failure is always a possibility, only those who don't fear failure can succeed.

5. Lastly, she mentions that those who do not fear failure look forward to going to work every day so they have a chance to make a positive difference in a patient's life. She leaves the reader with the thought that the applicant loves going to work. She ends with, "These are my beliefs. These are the reasons I want to be a PA." Her entire essay and her reasons for wanting to be a PA are summarized in these two brief sentences.

EXAMPLE 2

> The clinic may be like a zoo, but working there invigorates and challenges me. It's hard not to become resilient and quick thinking when so many things are happening at one time. Some people would go insane. When things are hectic, you learn to prioritize while always seeing the patient as the most important person in the room. Lei is my idea of the ideal PA. She is what I'd like to be, and given the opportunity, I will dedicate myself to patient care and to serving every patient whether rich, poor, an immigrant, a limited English speaker, or someone who is angry or has difficulty hearing. They all need the care of a physician assistant.

This is why this is a good conclusion:

1. The applicant summarizes what she said in her essay.

2. She began her essay with how hectic the emergency room was and how they had to prioritize. She mentions it again in her conclusion, which ties the essay together and demonstrates that she understands the need to prioritize.

3. She reminds the reader that she knows that when things are in chaos, we tend to begin thinking about our own priorities and lose sight of the patient. For this reason, PAs need to be resilient. Further, she reinforces the fact that the patient is the most important person in the room.

4. In the essay, the applicant talked about Lei, a PA she shadowed, and how Lei made her want to become a PA. She mentions her again in her conclusion. "She is what I'd like to be..."
5. She again ties the body of her essay to the conclusion when the applicant says she will serve every patient, whether rich or poor,

an immigrant, limited-English speaking, hard of hearing, or someone who is angry like a woman she mentioned in the body of her essay. It is these qualities she admired in Lei.

6. She concludes with a short sentence, "They all need the care of a physician assistant."

Get to Work: Eight Steps to Writing Your Personal Statement

Now that you know the basics, you're ready to write. Remember, writing is rewriting. Don't expect your first draft to be your final draft.

STEP 1: Sit Down and Write Your First Draft

Don't forget the old proverb, "Beginning is half done." At this stage, consider a general outline for the points you want to make.

Don't worry about punctuation, spelling, word count, descriptive words, too many words, not enough words, fragments, run-on sentences, etc. You just want to get your thoughts down on paper.

STEP 2: Read What You have Written and Let It Sit Overnight

Let your subconscious digest what you wrote. You'll have a fresh eye in the morning.

STEP 3: Edit One Paragraph at a Time

It's better to take small bites instead of one big one.

STEP 4: Break Your Essay up into Small Paragraphs

White space gives the eye a necessary break. Your essay will appear manageable to the admissions readers instead of overwhelming.

STEP 5: Cross Out, but Don't Delete Unnecessary Words

You might decide later you need some of what you crossed out. Or you might see something that sparks a new idea.

STEP 6: Reread Your Paragraph

If you need to strike more words, do so. Always keep your reader in mind as you write and rewrite. Readers don't want to wade through unnecessary words to get to the heart of your story. Then rewrite.

(This is a good place to make sure you've followed all instructions provided by CASPA or a particular PA school.)

STEP 7: Check Your Paragraph For Grammar, Spelling, And Punctuation

Do not do the following:

1) Use fragments (Fragments do not have a subject and a verb or don't express a complete thought.)

2) Write long run-on sentences (sentences that go on forever).

3) Use contractions (e.g. can't, wouldn't, doesn't etc.)

4) Sentences that:

    a. begin with a conjunction (e.g. and, but, also, etc.)
    b. end with a preposition (e.g. to, of, for, etc.)
    c. begin with a number (e.g starting a sentence with a 12 instead of Twelve)

5) Use incorrect punctuation:

Punctuate inside the quotation marks: "I find essay writing easy after reading these tips," Bill said.

STEP 8: Vary Sentence Length

Shorter sentences are better than longer ones, but too many short sentences will make your writing choppy. Too many long sentences put the reader to sleep.

REMINDERS

1. Show, don't tell. A picture is worth a thousand words.

2. Use active voice over passive voice. Example: "Bill hit the ball" instead of "The ball was hit by Bill."

3. Avoid run-on sentences. A short sentence is preferable over a longer one. There is one caveat to keep in mind. Short sentences are good, but too many short sentences in a row can make your essay choppy. Vary the sentence lengths.

4. Eliminate unnecessary words. Put yourself in the PA admission committee readers' place. Would you rather read a short, concise essay or a long rambling one? You know the answer.

5. Lastly, make sure every sentence and every paragraph is relevant. The measure of relevance is: "Will this paragraph make the PA admissions committee want to invite me for an interview?"

CHAPTER 3

Personal Statements

Unlocking the Mystery of Successful Personal Statements

"The funny thing about writing is that whether you're doing it well or doing it poorly, it looks exactly the same. That's actually one of the main ways that writing is different from ballet dancing."

– John Green

You've read what admission committee members are looking for in a competitive essay. You've learned the three basic building blocks of all essays — an introduction, body and conclusion. Now, you'll look at several example essays that resulted in PA school admissions.

Since beginning the essay collaborative in 2013, we have logged hundreds of hours reviewing, editing and collaborating with prospective PA students from across the country. Our candidates come from all walks of life, everything from professional dance instructors to recent college graduates, even practicing physicians looking to enter the PA profession.

A large majority of these candidates have been accepted into PA school.

Before and After the Anatomy of an Essay Edit

Editing is like surgery — you cut, sew, graft when necessary, and replace parts that don't work. Follow the surgery from pre-op to post-op of three winning essays. The essays are printed as submitted.to the *The PA Life Essay Collaborative.* All these applicants received interviews. Two of the three are currently in PA school.

Note: Remember, CASPA currently allows 5,000 characters, which includes spaces. Before submitting, though, always check for guideline updates. Requirements may change.

Essay 1

ORIGINAL ESSAY
3,587 characters with spaces

As the snowflakes fell on a cold winter day, the chills of the air were as somber as my feelings that day. As I stared out the window of the bus, I could only think to myself, "What happened?" "How did I get here?" I had just failed my freshman year of college, flunking every course except for my philosophy class because of a philosophy professor who never failed anyone.

In a small Korean hospital nestled in Kyonggi-Do, my biological mother gave birth to me. Most likely, young, afraid, and with little support in a Korean society that shames women who are pregnant out of wedlock, she decided to make the choice to give me up for adoption. I remained in foster care as an orphan for approximately 5 months and in 1985, a Caucasian family from rural Hudson, Wisconsin adopted me.

I was blessed, two other children who my adoptive parents attempted to get before me were so sick due to malnourishment in South Korea at the time that they couldn't make the flight. As a result, my family called me, "Lucky number 3." Growing up in a rural all Caucasian community where the biggest news was that a new dairy farm opened up wasn't easy. I tried to fit in as best as I could but as you probably know, people can be cruel. "Slanted eyes," "China man," and "How can you even see" were an all but common experience I would face every time I went to school. It raised many questions in my life later on such as: Why I had to go through this? Why would my 'real' mother abandon me?

Things didn't get any easier in my life. My adoptive parents divorced when I was only 4 years old and later on my step-dad and my mom divorced when I was 12. My step-dad was an alcoholic and abusive. After the second divorce, my sister and I moved back in with my dad where we both finished our remaining high school years.

As I entered my freshman year of college, I really was lost. I had no idea who I was, what I was passionate about, and what, if any, was my purpose in life. I sunk deeper into depression and contemplated suicide a few times. I began to stop attending my classes all together and would remain in my room for days on end.

So, as my bags were packed on a cold winter day, I headed back home with perhaps the same feelings my biological mom had felt, lost, afraid, and ashamed. For the next 3 years, I worked in various jobs trying to get by. During much of that time I thought I was wasting my time not going through the traditional finish college route but what I found was that I would find my purpose, my passion and meaning in the unlikeliest of places.

I took care of an older man who could hardly walk because he had cerebral palsy. Each time I helped him walk to the kitchen or bedroom he'd gaze at me with a wide smile that said, "You just made my day."

He had tremors at night so I often held him so he'd know I was there. Mark had difficulty speaking so he often shared pictures of his family. Many had passed away or were no longer part of this life.

The look he gave me that night was a loving, caring, and understanding one. Words no longer mattered except to describe that moment to my parents. When I looked into his eyes, I could feel him saying, "You understand me, you really care about me, thank you for taking the time to really hear my voice." That's the "voice" we all of us have deep inside. It seeks out these moments, where our motives no longer become self-seeking but other-seeking. In a world where we race around for the next best "thing" to satisfy us, these precious moments become cherished for what they are, bringing not the worst out of people but the best.

BREAKING IT DOWN PARAGRAPH BY PARAGRAPH

ORIGINAL: As the snowflakes fell on a cold winter day, the chills of the air were as somber as my feelings that day. As I stared out the window of the bus, I could only think to myself, "What happened?" "How did I get here?" I had just failed my freshman year of college, flunking every course except for my philosophy class because of a philosophy professor who never failed anyone.

REVISION: The snow and the chill on that cold winter day were as somber as my feelings as I stared out the bus window. I had just failed my freshman year of college, flunking every course except my philosophy class because the professor never failed anyone. "What happened and how did I get here?"

ORIGINAL: In a small Korean hospital nestled in Kyonggi-Do, my biological mother gave birth to me. Most likely, young, afraid, and with little support in a Korean society that shames women who are pregnant out of wedlock, she decided to make the choice to give me up for adoption. I remained in foster care as an orphan for approximately 5 months and in 1985, a Caucasian family from rural Hudson, Wisconsin adopted me.

REVISION: I was born in a small Korean hospital. My biological mom was young, afraid, and an outcast in a Korean society that shames women who are pregnant and unmarried. She gave me up for adoption, and I became a foster care orphan until a Caucasian family from rural Wisconsin adopted me in 1985.

ORIGINAL: I was blessed, two other children who my adoptive parents attempted to get before me were so sick due to malnourishment in South Korea at the time that they couldn't make the flight. As a result, my family called me, "Lucky number 3." Growing up in a rural all Caucasian community where the biggest news was that a new dairy farm opened up wasn't easy. I tried to fit in as best as I could but as you probably know, people can be cruel. "Slanted eyes," "China man," and "How can you even see" were an all but common experience I would face every time I went to school. It raised many questions in my life later on such as: Why I had to go through this? Why would my 'real' mother abandon me?

Things didn't get any easier in my life. My adoptive parents divorced when I was only 4 years old and later on my step-dad and my mom divorced when I was 12. My step-dad was an alcoholic and abusive. After the second divorce, my sister and I moved back in with my dad where we both finished our remaining high school years.

REVISION: We lived in a Caucasian community. "Slant eyes," "China man," and "How can you even see" were the taunts I faced every day at school. My adoptive parents divorced twice, but I managed to graduate from high school even though I moved over ten times.

ORIGINAL: As I entered my freshman year of college, I really was lost. I had no idea who I was, what I was passionate about, and what, if any, was my purpose in life. I sunk deeper into depression and contemplated suicide a few times. I began to stop attending my classes all together and would remain in my room for days on end.

So, as my bags were packed on a cold winter day, I headed back home with perhaps the same feelings my biological mom had felt, lost, afraid, and ashamed. For the next 3 years, I worked in various jobs trying to get by. During much of that time I thought I was wasting my time not going through the traditional finish college route but what I found was that I would find my purpose, my passion and meaning in the unlikeliest of places.

REVISION: I wondered if my biological mother felt as afraid, lost, and ashamed as I felt when the bus came to a stop and I walked down the steps to be embraced by my father, who made me realize everything would be all right.

Over the next three years I worked in various jobs and tried to get on with my life. A number of medical professionals worked with me to overcome the shame and fear I felt because of the debilitating effects of acne. I spent years reading about the human body and its ability to heal itself. I examined medical journals, read the latest articles on dermatology, and experimented in hopes of finding a cure. I eventually found an acne cure that worked for me, and made me realize how much I enjoyed learning about the human body.

ORIGINAL: I took care of an older man who could hardly walk because he had cerebral palsy. Each time I helped him walk to the kitchen or bedroom he'd gaze at me with a wide smile that said, "You just made my day." He had tremors at night so I often held him so he'd know I was there. Mark had difficulty speaking so he often shared pictures of his family. Many had passed away or were no longer part of this life.

REVISION: Then a fortunate thing happened. I found a job as a care-giver for three patients who had disabilities. One patient in particular changed the direction of my life and started me thinking about working in medicine.

I took care of an older man who could hardly walk because he had cerebral palsy. Mark had difficulty keeping his balance so I held his hand or supported him with my arms to steady him. He was terrified by night tremors, so I often held him until he fell asleep.

Mark cared deeply for his family and wanted to share their lives with me. He loved showing me pictures and writing down their names because he could no longer speak. After we were done, he gave me a look that changed my life.

ORIGINAL: The look he gave me that night was a loving, caring, and understanding one. Words no longer mattered except to describe that moment to my parents. When I looked into his eyes, I could feel him saying, "You understand me, you really care about me, thank you for taking the time to really hear my voice." That's the "voice" we all of us have deep inside. It seeks out these moments, where our motives no longer become self-seeking but other-seeking. In a world where we race around for the next best "thing" to satisfy us, these precious moments become cherished for what they are, bringing not the worst out of people but the best.

REVISION: His gentle eyes told me he just wanted to be loved, cared for, and understood. His bright smile confirmed that when we take the time to care for each other, it has the power to exponentially change that person's life and the lives of others.

While I thought I was helping Mark, it was Mark who was helping me. It is true that other patients helped me decide to go into medicine, but Mark had the biggest impact on my life.

I realized that a sincere connection with another human being can only be made when we take the time to listen to our patients and empathize with their needs. It is only then that we have the power to help them in the healing process. Patch Adams said, "You treat a disease, you win, you lose. You treat a person, I guarantee you you'll win, no matter what the outcome."

Soon after my experience with Mark, I went back to college, and graduated with a 3.78 GPA. I began to focus on helping others and developed two websites that give people a chance to share their life stories.

I want to be a physician assistant because it gives me an opportunity to use my life experience, medical knowledge, openness to new ideas, and passion for those who need a caring and compassionate person to help them when they are most vulnerable. It will enable me to honor patients like Mark, who made a difference in my life.

THE FINAL ESSAY
4,059 characters with spaces

The snow and the chill on that cold winter day were as somber as my feelings as I stared out the window of the bus. I had just failed my freshman year of college, flunking every course except my philosophy class because the professor never failed anyone. "What happened and how did I get there?"

I was born in a small Korean hospital. My biological mom was young, afraid, and an outcast in a Korean society that shames women who are pregnant and unmarried. She gave me up for adoption and I became a foster care orphan until a Caucasian family from rural Wisconsin adopted me in 1985.

We lived in a Caucasian community. "Slant eyes," "China man," and "How can you even see" were the taunts I faced every day at school. My adoptive parents divorced twice, but I managed to graduate from high school even though I moved over ten times.

I wondered if my biological mother felt as afraid, lost, and ashamed as I felt when the bus came to a stop, and I walked down the steps to be embraced by my father, who made me realize everything would be all right.

Over the next three years I worked in various jobs and tried to get on with my life. A number of medical professionals worked with me to overcome the shame and fear I felt because of the debilitating effects of acne. I spent years reading about the human body and its ability to heal itself. I examined medical journals, read the latest articles on dermatology, and experimented in hopes of finding a cure for my acne. I eventually found a cure that worked for me and made me realize how much I enjoyed learning about the human body.

Then a fortunate thing happened. I found a job as a caregiver for three patients who had disabilities. One patient in particular changed the direction of my life and started me thinking about working in medicine.

I took care of an older man who could hardly walk because he had cerebral palsy. Mark had difficulty keeping his balance so I held his hand or supported him with my arms to steady him. He was terrified by night tremors, so I often held him until he fell asleep.

Mark cared deeply for his family and wanted to share their lives with me. He loved showing me pictures and writing down their names because he could no longer speak. After we were done, he gave me a look that changed my life.

His gentle eyes told me he just wanted to be loved, cared for, and understood. His bright smile confirmed that when we take the time to care for each other, it has the power to exponentially change that person's life and the lives of others.

While I thought I was helping Mark, it was Mark who was helping me. It is true that other patients helped me decide to go into medicine, but Mark had the biggest impact on my life.

I realized that a sincere connection with another human being can only be made when we take the time to listen to our patients and empathize with their needs; it is only then that we have the power to help them in the healing process. Patch Adams said, "You treat a disease, you win, you lose. You treat a person, I guarantee you you'll win, no matter what the outcome."

Soon after my experience with Mark, I went back to college, and graduated with a 3.78 GPA. I began to focus on helping others and developed two websites that give people a chance to share their life stories.

I want to be a physician assistant because it gives me an opportunity to use my life experience, medical knowledge, openness to new ideas, and passion for those who need a caring and compassionate person to help them when they are most vulnerable. It will enable me to honor patients like Mark, who made a difference in my life.

Essay 2

ORIGINAL ESSAY
4,990 characters with spaces

The turning point in my life was winter quarter 2012 at UC Davis; I took anatomy and interned at the UC Davis Medical Center's Cardiac Rehabilitation Department. The anatomy lab was a cadaver lab. I spent much more than the minimum hours required there and learned that I had a stronger stomach than I had thought. I enjoyed it so much I barely noticed how many hours of studying it demanded. Meanwhile during my internship, I met a Physician Assistant who would stop by to chat with the nurses. This was the first time I became aware that Physician Assistants existed. While memorizing the anatomy of the heart, I received a phone call from my internship, "We have an opportunity for you to observe an aortic valve replacement surgery." I was giddy and nervous at once. Normally I worked in an outpatient setting, taking resting and exercise blood pressures and heart rates of patients who previously had cardiac surgeries or were at risk for having a heart attack. I held cadaver hearts before but now I was going to see a live heart! I immediately searched aortic valve replacement surgeries on YouTube for preparation. Even with my research, I was still anxious; I had never been in an operating room before except for my birth. Prior to the surgery, I was told "relax, breathe, and if you feel like you're going to faint, it's okay. We've had nurses, technicians, and medical students faint. Just sit down immediately." All I could think was "Great, everyone faints. I'm going to faint."

But ten hours and two surgeries later, I never fainted! In fact, I was intrigued and fascinated. I asked as many questions as I could without disrupting. I learned how each job involved was meticulous and important. I even leaned over the patient by the anesthesiologist and saw the patient's heart up close! I also observed a coronary artery bypass graft when a nurse mentioned something to me that caught my attention "The PA over there is harvesting the vein."

The PA? I was hearing that title more and more, in the operating room, in outpatient cardiac rehab, and in my own doctor's office. After witnessing my first two surgeries, I immediately began researching a career as a PA. What attracted me about PA's was that they were not limited to one area of medicine. That summer I shadowed a General Surgery PA to learn directly what it was like to be a PA. He was precepting PA students at the time and learning alongside them cemented my passion for choosing PA.

I am now working as an EMT, and although we take heart rates, blood pressures, and administer oxygen, it feels different than any other clinical experience I've had. As a transport EMT, most of our patients are stable, so I don't provide treatment as much as I provide patience, compassion, and understanding. On many occasions, the only treatment I have provided was a hand to hold or an ear to listen. One day we were transporting a patient to her doctor's appointment and back to her nursing home, a fairly standard transport, or so I thought. The patient had an extremely rare disease called Systemic Scleroderma. She began explaining her disease to me, and I told her I actually knew a fair amount about it as I had done a research project on Scleroderma and Morphea in college because of a friend struggling with Morphea. She was so surprised and thrilled that I knew about it and she admitted to me that most nurses she deals with don't know the disease because of its rarity, and with tears in her eyes she opened up to me describing her struggle. She told me it took a long time just to be diagnosed. People didn't think she was really sick because she can hid it with makeup and clothes, but her skin is hard and the pain is horrible. She said "people thought I was one of those people just trying to get meds, but I was in so much pain so of course the first thing I wanted was pain medicine." It was true she didn't look very sick; her hands were a little disfigured and her feet wrapped in bandages but other than that she looked fairly normal. She told me horror stories of pain from blood draws, PICC lines and portacaths due to her tough skin and tissue. I listened to her story, and often she would tear up and repeat "people just don't understand." I let her know I understood. I loved how she opened up to me and when we brought her back to the nursing facility I told her I would look for her if I was ever back there again and she replied "you'd better!" It was the first time I have ever been able to combine my science knowledge from college and my ability to provide understanding and care for someone. I felt as though I got a taste of what it would be like to be a PA. I love learning about science and health but more than that, I want to be able to put my knowledge to work. I want to explore health care with my ready-to-learn enthusiasm for science while also using my compassion to care for people like they are more than an anatomy textbook. My experiences have made me more excited to become a PA.

BREAKING IT DOWN PARAGRAPH BY PARAGRAPH

ORIGINAL: The turning point in my life was winter quarter 2012 at UC Davis; I took anatomy and interned at the UC Davis Medical Center's Cardiac Rehabilitation Department. The anatomy lab was a cadaver lab. I spent much more than the minimum hours required there and learned that I had a stronger stomach than I had thought. I enjoyed it so much I barely noticed how many hours of studying it demanded. Meanwhile during my internship, I met a Physician Assistant who would stop by to chat with the nurses. This was the first time I became aware that Physician Assistants existed. While memorizing the anatomy of the heart, I received a phone call from my internship, "We have an opportunity for you to observe an aortic valve replacement surgery." I was giddy and nervous at once. Normally I worked in an outpatient setting, taking resting and exercise blood pressures and heart rates of patients who previously had cardiac surgeries or were at risk for having a heart attack. I held cadaver hearts before but now I was going to see a live heart! I immediately searched aortic valve replacement surgeries on YouTube for preparation. Even with my research, I was still anxious; I had never been in an operating room before except for my birth. Prior to the surgery, I was told "relax, breathe, and if you feel like you're going to faint, it's okay. We've had nurses, technicians, and medical students faint. Just sit down immediately." All I could think was "Great, everyone faints. I'm going to faint."

REVISION: Many experiences led me to the decision to become a physician assistant, but three experiences stand out above the rest: Shirley, a patient I met while working as an EMT, an open heart surgery that lasted ten hours, and the summer I shadowed a PA.

The limited understanding I had about the intricacies of patient care prior to deciding to become a PA soon changed after my experience working as an EMT. While our job involves checking heart rates, blood pressure, and oxygen levels, it is different from other clinical experiences I've had. I learned the importance of listening, patience, compassion, and understanding on a day that started like every other.

ORIGINAL: But ten hours and two surgeries later, I never fainted! In fact, I was intrigued and fascinated. I asked as many questions as I could without disrupting. I learned how each job involved was meticulous and important. I even leaned over the patient by the anesthesiologist and saw the patient's heart up close! I also observed a coronary artery bypass graft when a nurse mentioned something to me that caught my attention "The PA over there is harvesting the vein."

The PA? I was hearing that title more and more, in the operating room, in outpatient cardiac rehab, and in my own doctor's office. After witnessing my first two surgeries, I immediately began researching a career as a PA. What attracted me about PA's was that they were not limited to one area of medicine. That summer I shadowed a General Surgery PA to

5 58

learn directly what it was like to be a PA. He was precepting PA students at the time and learning alongside them cemented my passion for choosing PA.

REVISION: Part of my job was to transport patients to their doctor's appointment and back to the nursing home. Shirley was one of our former patients. She had an extremely rare disease, Systemic Scleroderma. She was fifty-one and stood out from the regular nursing home tenants. Shirley always fixed herself up like she was ready for a night on the town. Her smooth black skin did not show her age. Shirley wore shimmering gold lip gloss that matched the golden weave that curled into a perfect bun on top of her head. By contrast, her fingers were shorter than usual and they seemed more like claws than hands because she had trouble gripping and bending the joints. The skin on her hands were as tight as the skin on her face and ears. I soon realized that was why she did not have many wrinkles. Her feet were wrapped in bandages and she said she had "ulcers" that caused her extreme pain

I had previously researched Systemic Scleroderma and was able to easily empathize with her as I talked with her and listened to her describe her experience with non medical people as well as treatment providers who thought she was not sick because she hid her symptoms with makeup and clothes.

"My skin is hard and the pain is horrible," she said. "People think I am trying to get meds, but I was in so much pain, medicine was the first thing I needed." She shared horror stories of pain from blood draws and PICC lines and portacaths due to her tough skin and tissue. Shirley teared up as I listened to her story. It was obvious the lack of understanding she receives bothered her more than the mortality of the disease. She kept saying, "Thank you so much for listening and caring." When we had her settled back in the nursing home, she said, "Please come back and see me again." I promised her I would.

I returned to her nursing facility before work a few weeks later, and brought her a small bouquet of flowers. She gave me a hug and started crying when she saw the flowers. "You don't know how much I needed this, I've been sicker lately and this brightened my day." We sat on her bed and talked. The conversation picked up as if it had only been a day since I'd last seen her. When I listened and showed understanding, Shirley opened up to me and I learned things about her I may not have known otherwise, I will take this lesson with me when I become a PA.

ORIGINAL: But ten hours and two surgeries later, I never fainted! In fact, I was intrigued and fascinated. I asked as many questions as I could without disrupting. I learned how each job involved was meticulous and important. I even leaned over the patient by the anesthesiologist and saw the patient's heart up close! I also observed a coronary artery bypass graft when a nurse mentioned something to me that caught my attention "The PA over there is harvesting the vein."

The PA? I was hearing that title more and more, in the operating room, in outpatient cardiac rehab, and in my own doctor's office. After witnessing my first two surgeries, I immediately began researching a career as a PA. What attracted me about PA's was that they were not limited to one area of medicine. That summer I shadowed a General Surgery PA to learn directly what it was like to be a PA. He was precepting PA students at the time and learning alongside them cemented my passion for choosing PA.

I am now working as an EMT, and although we take heart rates, blood pressures, and administer oxygen, it feels different than any other clinical experience I've had. As a transport EMT, most of our patients are stable, so I don't provide treatment as much as I provide patience, compassion, and understanding. On many occasions, the only treatment I have provided was a hand to hold or an ear to listen. One day we were transporting a patient to her doctor's appointment and back to her nursing home, a fairly standard transport, or so I thought. The patient had an extremely rare disease called Systemic Scleroderma. She began explaining her disease to me, and I told her I actually knew a fair amount about it as I had done a research project on Scleroderma and Morphea in college because of a friend struggling with Morphea. She was so surprised and thrilled that I knew about it and she admitted to me that most nurses she deals with don't know the disease because of its rarity, and with tears in her eyes she opened up to me describing her struggle. She told me it took a long time just to be diagnosed. People didn't think she was really sick because she can hid it with makeup and clothes, but her skin is hard and the pain is horrible. She said "people thought I was one of those people just trying to get meds, but I was in so much pain so of course the first thing I wanted was pain medicine." It was true she didn't look very sick; her hands were a little disfigured and her feet wrapped in bandages but other than that she looked fairly normal. She told me horror stories of pain from blood draws, PICC lines and portacaths due to her tough skin and tissue. I listened to her story, and often she would tear up and repeat "people just don't understand." I let her know I understood. I loved how she opened up to me and when we brought her back to the nursing facility I told her I would look for her if I was ever back there again and she replied "you'd better!" It was the first time I have ever been able to combine my science knowledge from college and my ability to provide understanding and care for someone. I felt as though I got a taste of what it would be like to be a PA. I love learning about science and health but more than that, I want to be able to put my knowledge to work. I want to explore health care with my ready-to-learn enthusiasm for science while also using my compassion to care for people like they are more than an anatomy textbook. My experiences have made me more excited to become a PA.

REVISION: The second thing that influenced my decision to become a PA took place when I was given the opportunity to observe an aortic valve replacement surgery. My fascination from the first buzz of the saw to suturing the chest never wavered through ten hours and two surgeries.

During the coronary bypass graft in the second surgery, a nurse casually mentioned, "That's a PA harvesting the vein."

Before that, I did not realize PAs could specialize in many areas of medicine. This appealed to me, so I began exploring a career as a physician assistant. That summer I shadowed, Sean, a general surgery PA, who was responsible for supervising PA students while they were doing their clinical rotations. I kept a list of every type of surgery I saw, and often went home with a list of new diseases to research. Sean's PA students were physiology lovers like myself. They loved learning new things and applying their knowledge. Their enthusiasm was unmatched by anyone I had met in any other clinical setting. Learning alongside them cemented my desire to become a PA.

We never know which of our life experiences will cause us to choose one career over another. These three experiences are the reason I chose to be a PA. Shirley's smile and tears when she saw the flowers made me realize just how much something so small could mean so much. Spending ten hours in surgery and finding out that PAs can be a part of that, made my desire to be a PA even stronger. The enthusiasm of the PA students that worked with Sean made me want to become a part of a medical team and realize becoming a PA was right for me.

THE FINAL ESSAY
4,613 characters with spaces

Many experiences led me to the decision to become a physician assistant, but three experiences stand out above the rest: Shirley, a patient I met while working as an EMT, an open heart surgery that lasted ten hours, and the summer I shadowed a PA.

The limited understanding I had about the intricacies of patient care prior to deciding to become a PA soon changed after my experience working as an EMT. While our job involves checking heart rates, blood pressure, and oxygen levels, it is different from other clinical experiences I've had. I learned the importance of listening, patience, compassion, and understanding on a day that started like every other.

Part of my job is to transport patients to their doctor's appointment and back to the nursing home. Shirley was one of our former patients. She had an extremely rare disease, systemic scleroderma. She was fifty-one and stood out from the regular nursing home tenants. Shirley always fixed herself up like she was ready for a night on the town. Her smooth black skin did not show her age. Shirley wore shimmering gold lip gloss that matched the golden weave that curled into a perfect bun on top of her head. By contrast, her fingers were shorter than usual and they seemed more like claws than hands because she had trouble gripping and bending the joints. The skin on her hands was as tight as the skin on her face and ears. I soon realized that was why she did not have many wrinkles. Her feet were wrapped in bandages and she said she had "ulcers" that caused her extreme pain.

I had previously researched systemic scleroderma and was able to easily empathize with her as I talked with her and listened to her describe her experience with non-medical people as well as treatment providers who thought she was not sick because she hid her symptoms with makeup and clothes.

"My skin is hard and the pain is horrible," she said. "People thought I was trying to get meds, but I was in so much pain, medicine was the first thing I needed." She shared horror stories of pain from blood draws and PICC lines and portacaths due to her tough skin and tissue. Shirley teared up as she told me her story. It was obvious the lack of understanding she receives bothered her more than the mortality of the disease. She kept saying, "Thank you so much for listening and caring." When we had her settled back in the nursing home, she said, "Please come back and see me again." I promised her I would.

I returned to her nursing facility before work a few weeks later and brought her a small bouquet of flowers. She gave me a hug and started crying when she saw the flowers. "You don't know how much I needed this, I've been sicker lately and this brightened my day." We sat on her bed and talked. The conversation picked up as if it had only been a day since I'd last seen her. When I listened and showed understanding, Shirley opened up to me and I learned things about her I may not have known otherwise. I will take this lesson with me when I become a PA.

The second thing that influenced my decision to become a PA took place when I was given the opportunity to observe an aortic valve replacement surgery. My fascination from the first buzz of the saw to suturing the chest never wavered through ten hours and two surgeries. During the coronary bypass graft in the second surgery, a nurse casually mentioned, "That's a PA harvesting the vein."

Before that, I did not realize PAs could specialize in many areas of medicine. This appealed to me, so I began exploring a career as a physician assistant. That summer I shadowed Sean, a general surgery PA, who was responsible for supervising PA students while they were doing their clinical rotations. I kept a list of every type of surgery I saw and often went home with a list of new diseases to research. Sean's PA students were physiology lovers like myself. They loved learning new things and applying their knowledge. Their enthusiasm was unmatched by anyone I'd met in any other clinical setting. Learning alongside them cemented my desire to become a PA.

We never know which of our life experiences will cause us to choose one career over another. These three experiences are the reason I chose to be a PA. Shirley's smile and tears when she saw the flowers made me realize just how much something so small could mean so much. Spending ten hours in surgery and finding out that PAs can be a part of that, made my desire to be a PA even stronger. The enthusiasm of the PA students that worked with Sean made me want to become a part of a medical team and realize becoming a PA was right for me.

Essay 3

ORIGINAL
4,489 characters with spaces

During my second week at the After Hour Kids (AHK) clinic, I sat with Justin, an 11-year-old having difficulty breathing. His family was obviously distraught as we struggled to raise his pulse oximetry reading. I calmly explained the treatments we were administering through the nebulizer and that while his breathing was more deeply than before, we needed to arrange transport to an emergency department. This would allow for further observation and an increased scope of care than we could provide at our facility. After we escorted them with the paramedics to the ambulance and they were in route, I realized how nervous I was as I finally exhaled; it was a feeling that took me back to years before.

At the young age of nine, I decided I wanted to play volleyball. Perhaps it was watching my brother, 13 years my senior, play in college. I marveled at how high the players could jump and how fast the ball seemed to move in my young eyes. I told him, "I want to play volleyball." Excitedly, he began my training in my backyard. All we did was practice forearm passing and footwork. We did this day after day over the summer and when he was home on the weekends. I kept asking when we would get to practice spiking the ball. He said, "Not yet. If you can do this, you can play with anyone, anywhere." That was the day I learned fundamentals.

Fortunately, I heeded his advice. Several months later while attending my first volleyball camp I was approached to play for a top local club in the Under 12s division. I was overwhelmed with excitement but also very intimidated. As I was dropped off alone at my first practice, I realized how much taller everyone was compared to me. I calmed myself by remembering all the work I had put in, concentrating on the process of passing and defense, and became entrenched in the moment. The hard work reaped dividends. Eventually, I would go to nationals six times, become the first freshman to start the high school varsity squad, be voted Captain by my peers, and receive recruitment attention by numerous Division II and III schools. I did all this and I am barely 5'4".

While my brother is over 6'3, it became obvious early in my playing career I wasn't going to be in a similar height percentile. Distraught at times, I always fell back on my work ethic. Sports are not always about the most talented or gifted. They are often stories of leadership, hard work, and perseverance. Through my intense study of the game I became a leader as I guided us from the backcourt. I became increasingly adept at not only learning the habits and behaviors of opponents but as a leader I needed to also understand the psychology of my teammates. This was an important skill not only during matches but during practice as I helped teach and train those around me. And although I was always nervous before a match, I took comfort in my process as a player and knew every time I stepped onto the court I worked as hard and efficiently as I could have for today. Knowing that brought me a sense of calm and focus.

As I watched the ambulance pull away I realized the long journey in front of me. I began viewing my job as a medical assistant through the eyes of a team member. While the University of Texas offered me an increased intellectual understanding of the science underpinning medical decisions, I challenged myself to learn the tools and processes to increase the efficiency of the office and the overall patient experience. Whether it's requesting to learn the front office duties or shadowing the RNs to gain a direct understanding of their workload, I make every effort to analyze processes that will improve the patient's experience. While I truly enjoy interacting with patients and being an integral part of a medical team, I also want to be in a position to provide a higher level of care.

Physician Assistant school will provide me with an opportunity to increase both my theoretical knowledge as well as practical experience in an environment surrounded by other highly motivated individuals with similar goals.

A couple of days after Justin went to the hospital I followed up with a phone call to his family to make sure he was doing okay. His parents repeatedly thanked me again and expressed sincere thankfulness at not only the care we provided but for keeping them calm and informed during the process. While I will always enjoy my memories of volleyball and everything it taught me, that moment was worth a thousand trips to Nationals.

BREAKING IT DOWN PARAGRAPH BY PARAGRAPH

ORIGINAL OPENING: During my second week at the After Hour Kids (AHK) clinic, I sat with Justin, an 11-year-old having difficulty breathing. His family was obviously distraught as we struggled to raise his pulse oximetry reading. I calmly explained the treatments we were administering through the nebulizer and that while his breathing was more deeply than before, we needed to arrange transport to an emergency department. This would allow for further observation and an increased scope of care than we could provide at our facility. After we escorted them with the paramedics to the ambulance and they were in route, I realized how nervous I was as I finally exhaled; it was a feeling that took me back to years before.

Three long paragraphs followed the opening

At the young age of nine, I decided I wanted to play volleyball. Perhaps it was watching my brother, 13 years my senior, play in college. I marveled at how high the players could jump and how fast the ball seemed to move in my young eyes. I told him, "I want to play volleyball." Excitedly, he began my training in my backyard. All we did was practice forearm passing and footwork. We did this day after day over the summer and when he was home on the weekends. I kept asking when we would get to practice spiking the ball. He said, "Not yet. If you can do this, you can play with anyone, anywhere." That was the day I learned fundamentals.

Fortunately, I heeded his advice. Several months later while attending my first volleyball camp I was approached to play for a top local club in the Under 12s division. I was overwhelmed with excitement but also very intimidated. As I was dropped off alone at my first practice, I realized how much taller everyone was compared to me. I calmed myself by remembering all the work I had put in, concentrating on the process of passing and defense, and became entrenched in the moment. The hard work reaped dividends. Eventually, I would go to nationals six times, become the first freshman to start the high school varsity squad, be voted Captain by my peers, and receive recruitment attention by numerous Division II and III schools. I did all this and I am barely 5'4".

While my brother is over 6'3, it became obvious early in my playing career I wasn't going to be in a similar height percentile. Distraught at times, I always fell back on my work ethic. Sports are not always about the most talented or gifted. They are often stories of leadership, hard work, and perseverance. Through my intense study of the game I became a leader as I guided us from the backcourt. I became increasingly adept at not only learning the habits and behaviors of opponents but as a leader I needed to also understand the psychology of my teammates. This was an important skill not only during matches but during practice as I helped teach and train those around me. And although I was always nervous before a match, I took comfort in my process as a player and knew every time I stepped onto the court I worked as hard and efficiently as I could have for today. Knowing that brought me a sense of calm and focus.

REVISION: I decided at age nine that I wanted to play volleyball after watching my older brother play in college. I marveled at how high the players could jump and how fast the ball moved. My training began the day I told my brother I wanted to play volleyball. He insisted I learn the fundamentals first even though I desired to do everything right away. Months later I was given the opportunity to play for a top local club in the under 12 division. I was thrilled but also very intimidated. Everyone was much taller—I stood barely chest high to most of the girls.

It was obvious I'd never have the height of most players so I fell back on my work ethic. What I learned was that sports are not always about the most talented or gifted; rather they're about leadership, hard work, and perseverance which led to my playing on six teams that went to Nationals. An injury to my brother's rotator cuff spurred my interest in pursuing a career in medicine. I wanted to help him heal. When I first investigated possible medical jobs I didn't know medicine would become my passion. I soon discovered I loved it more than anything I had ever done.

ORIGINAL: During my second week at the After Hour Kids (AHK) clinic, I sat with Justin, an 11-year-old having difficulty breathing. His family was obviously distraught as we struggled to raise his pulse oximetry reading. I calmly explained the treatments we were administering through the nebulizer and that while his breathing was more deeply than before, we needed to arrange transport to an emergency department. This would allow for further observation and an increased scope of care than we could provide at our facility. After we escorted them with the paramedics to the ambulance and they were in route, I realized how nervous I was as I finally exhaled; it was a feeling that took me back to years before.

REVISION: During my second week at the After Hours Kids' Clinic, I sat with Justin, an 11-year old with breathing difficulties. He'd come in with his mom, still dressed in his neon blue soccer uniform. Justin's face was pale, his breathing wheezy and shallow. He sat rigidly on the exam table with his hands gripping his knees. His mom's lips trembled as she blinked back tears. She said this had never happened before and had no idea what precipitated it. I tried to comfort Justin by rubbing his back. After a few minutes, I felt him relax.

ORIGINAL: As I watched the ambulance pull away I realized the long journey in front of me. I began viewing my job as a medical assistant through the eyes of a team member. While the University of Texas offered me an increased intellectual understanding of the science underpinning medical decisions, I challenged myself to learn the tools and processes to increase the efficiency of the office and the overall patient experience. Whether it's requesting to learn the front office duties or shadowing the RNs to gain a direct understanding of their workload, I make every effort to analyze processes that will improve the patient's experience. While I truly enjoy interacting with patients and being an integral part of a medical team, I also want to be in a position to provide a higher level of care. Physician Assistant school will provide me with an opportunity to increase both my theoretical knowledge as well as practical experience in an environment surrounded by other highly motivated individuals with similar goals.

REVISION: Emily, the nurse practitioner, had me set Justin up on the pulse oximeter and we started nebulizer treatments. Despite the treatment, we only succeeded in raising his blood oxygen levels to 88%. Emily asked me to stay with Justin and his mom while she stepped out to call an ambulance.

I calmly explained that while the treatments had helped, we needed to get him to the hospital in an ambulance. I knew I had succeeded in making it fun instead of scary when he smiled and asked, "Will they turn on the sirens?" This made his mom smile for the first time since they'd walked into the clinic.

Although my volleyball career has ended, I use what I learned daily. Instead of reading my opponents, I assess my patient's needs. Each requires something different. Sometimes a patient needs a hand to hold or a distraction to keep their mind focused elsewhere during a procedure. Often they want someone to take more time to discuss their concerns.

While my education offered me an intellectual understanding of the science behind medical decisions, I challenged myself to learn more about clinic operations. I learned the front office duties so I could help during busy times. I also shadowed the RNs to gain a better understanding of their workload and increase my ability to effectively communicate with patients. I heed the advice my brother gave me when I was nine on a daily basis, "work hard and learn the fundamentals." In my role as a medical assistant I'm still a team player and it has helped me earn the trust of the medical staff.

While I enjoy my job as a medical assistant, I want to be able to provide a higher level of care, interact with patients, and be an integral part of a medical team. After shadowing a PA, I knew it was the job I had been seeking all along.

ORIGINAL: A couple of days after Justin went to the hospital I followed up with a phone call to his family to make sure he was doing okay. His parents repeatedly thanked me again and expressed sincere thankfulness at not only the care we provided but for keeping them calm and informed during the process. While I will always enjoy my memories of volleyball and everything it taught me, that moment was worth a thousand trips to Nationals.

REVISION: A couple of days after Justin went to the hospital I called his mom to make sure he was okay. She repeatedly thanked me not only for the care we provided, but for keeping them calm and informed during the process. I will always enjoy my memories of volleyball, but that moment with Justin and his mom was worth a thousand trips to Nationals.

THE FINAL ESSAY
3,785 characters with spaces

I decided at age nine that I wanted to play volleyball after watching my older brother play in college. I marveled at how high the players could jump and how fast the ball moved. My training began the day I told my brother I wanted to play volleyball. He insisted I learn the fundamentals first even though I desired to do everything right away. Months later I was given the opportunity to play for a top local club in the under 12 division. I was thrilled but also very intimidated. Everyone was much taller — I stood barely chest high to most of the girls.

It was obvious I'd never have the height of most players so I fell back on my work ethic. What I learned was that sports are not always about the most talented or gifted; rather they're about leadership, hard work, and perseverance which led to my playing on six teams that went to Nationals. An injury to my brother's rotator cuff spurred my interest in pursuing a career in medicine. I wanted to help him heal. When I first investigated possible medical jobs, I didn't know medicine would become my passion. I soon discovered I loved it more than anything I had ever done.

During my second week at the After Hours Kids' Clinic, I sat with Justin, an 11-year old with breathing difficulties. He'd come in with his mom, still dressed in his neon blue soccer uniform. Justin's face was pale, his breathing wheezy and shallow. He sat rigidly on the exam table with his hands gripping his knees. His mom's lips trembled as she blinked back tears. She said this had never happened before and had no idea what precipitated it. I tried to comfort Justin by rubbing his back. After a few minutes, I felt him relax.

Emily, the nurse practitioner, had me set Justin up on the pulse oximeter and we started nebulizer treatments. Despite the treatment, we only succeeded in raising his blood oxygen levels to 88%. Emily asked me to stay with Justin and his mom while she stepped out to call an ambulance.

I calmly explained that while the treatments had helped, we needed to get him to the hospital in an ambulance. I knew I had succeeded in making it fun instead of scary when he smiled and asked, "Will they turn on the sirens?" This made his mom smile for the first time since they'd walked into the clinic.

Although my volleyball career has ended, I use what I learned daily. Instead of reading my opponents, I assess my patient's needs. Each requires something different. Sometimes a patient needs a hand to hold or a distraction to keep their mind focused elsewhere during a procedure. Often they want someone to take more time to discuss their concerns.

While my education offered me an intellectual understanding of the science behind medical decisions, I challenged myself to learn more about clinic operations. I learned the front office duties so I could help during busy times. I also shadowed the RNs to gain a better understanding of their workload and increase my ability to effectively communicate with patients. I heed the advice my brother gave me when I was nine on a daily basis, "work hard and learn the fundamentals." In my role as a medical assistant I'm still a team player and it has helped me earn the trust of the medical staff.

While I enjoy my job as a medical assistant, I want to be able to provide a higher level of care, interact with patients, and be an integral part of a medical team. After shadowing a PA, I knew it was the job I had been seeking all along.

A couple of days after Justin went to the hospital I called his mom to make sure he was okay. She repeatedly thanked me not only for the care we provided, but for keeping them calm and informed during the process.

I will always enjoy my memories of volleyball, but that moment with Justin and his mom was worth a thousand trips to Nationals.

CHAPTER 4

Wrapping Up

"It always seems impossible until it's done."

– Nelson Mandela

To finish up this book we want to talk to you about a word that keeps many would-be successful PA school applicants from achieving their goal of writing a winning personal statement.

It is a tiny word with gigantic significance and one which you must overcome if you want to write a personal statement that resonates with the admissions committee.

What is this word?

FEAR

Often we'll blame our fear of writing on a lack of inspiration, poor genetics or writer's block, which may well be the case on some days. More often than not, we're unaware of our fear and disguise it as something else.

The fear we're talking about doesn't have to do with writer's block or lack of a "creativity chromosome." It's about believing in ourselves and believing we have something worthwhile to say.

COMPARISON - The Thief of a Meaningful Essay

When we doubt ourselves or the worth of our life experiences, we lose faith in our words. When we lose faith in our words, it's a pretty safe bet that we're comparing their value to the words of others.

Maybe you have read through the sample essays in this book or online, and now, when you look at what you have written, it appears elementary or just doesn't measure up to other essays.

Comparison is deadly, yet it seems to be inherent in human nature. If we look at what others have done or what others have to say and value it above our own work or experiences, we create a barrier between the page and our authentic words.

The healthiest type of comparison is to compare our work with our previous efforts and try to build on that. Keep in mind that the essays in this book have been edited and reedited through The PA Collaborative.

Take Risks

When we sit down to write our essay, we take a risk.

- We risk our words being rejected.
- We risk our work being compared to others.
- We risk revealing parts of ourselves we may not want others to see.
- We risk money, time with our loved ones, or worse yet, proving the naysayers right.

That's the nature of creating something meaningful; we're trading our time for the pursuit of something bigger than ourselves. Sharing a part of ourselves and sharing who we are is always risky because it makes us vulnerable.

But we keep going, encouraged by our goal of becoming a PA and ignited by our passion to serve.

That doesn't mean we'll always deliver according to expectations, be it the admissions committee's, or our own.

Writing Through Your Fear

Writing a meaningful essay takes courage.

If you're passionate about ballroom dance (like one of our candidates), you're going to inspire others to be passionate about ballroom dance. Your best work is where your passion lies.

With passion comes emotion. And with emotion comes vulnerability. It is where passion and emotion meet that the essay takes shape.

This doesn't mean if you are passionate about ballroom dancing you are going to write an entire essay about the ins-and-outs of the foxtrot and submit that to the admissions committee. It is your job to draw the parallels between your passion and your purpose and use this to frame your essay. It will provide the structure you need to reveal the human behind the grades, shadowing, volunteer work and healthcare experience.

If you embrace openness in your personal statement, you've done the best you can. Your only responsibility is to say what's in your heart and be true to yourself, the admissions committee, and your subject.

After that, the world (and the admissions committee) can do what it likes with your words.

The Personal Statement Collaborative

"You write to communicate to the hearts and minds of others what's burning inside you, and we edit to let the fire show through the smoke.

- Arthur Plotnik

This book is a byproduct of our time and experience working with hundreds of PA school applicants through our personal statement collaborative. For many well intentioned applicants, parents are often the first choice of proofreaders. Since the authors of this book are all parents, we applaud your decision to include family and/or friends in the application process. When it comes to your personal statement, family and friends don't always make the best editorial team. Your essay needs more than the sympathetic feedback provided by a friendly relative, who will be too critical or not critical enough.

Consider using our essay editing service to polish your essay

Read more about our service at www.thepaessay.com.

Here is what some of our customers have had to say

"I just wanted to take the time to comment on the services I received from the PA Life. I was extremely stressed out about writing my personal statement, and finally decided to search the internet for advice and assistance. I came across the statement editing service on the PA Life, and decided to give it a try. I received a response within a day or so, and my stress was instantly relieved. I worked personally with Duke to edit my statement, and he is a phenomenal writer. He didn't change the content of my statement, but rather helped me tell my story in a way that is much more desirable! I cannot recommend this service enough to others seeking help on their personal statement. Duke was friendly, sincere, and definitely experienced! I felt 100% confident in his editing abilities, and we worked together the entire time so that we were both pleased with the results! Thanks again, Duke, for all of your help!"

- Chelsie, K

"I wanted to give a brief update: I have had 4 interviews, 2 acceptances, 1 wait-list, and waiting on one more. Right now I have a deposit down at Univ. of Texas Medical Branch. Thanks for all your help. It really did make a difference, and I was even complimented on my narrative during a few interviews."

-Andrew S. PA-S

"I have recently been accepted to a program that was one of my top choices, and I also was waitlisted with two other schools. I wanted to thank you again for all your help. Not only am I grateful for your knowledge of writing and grammar (which were invaluable), but most importantly your kind words and motivation, which I needed so much at the time."

-Alex Taylor, PA-S

A Very Special Thanks To Our Contributors

1. Terry O'Donnell, BS, MAT, MHS, Associate Professor and Chair of Physician Assistant Studies at Quinnipiac University.

2. Lori Palfreyman, MS, Faculty Chair of the Admissions Committee at Rutgers University PA Program.

3. Tim Quigley, MPH, PA-C, Director of Student Affairs at MEDEX NW Division of Physician Assistant Studies.

4. Darwin Brown, MPH, PA-C, Associate Program Director and Director of Clinical Education at UNMC.

5. Wayne Stuart, MD, Director, DeSales University Physician Assistant Program.

6. Grace Landel, MEd, PA-C, Program Director Joint MSPAS/MPH Program, Touro University California.

7. Audra Perrino, MS, Director of Admissions at Stony Brook School of Health Technology and Management.

8. Judith Stallings, EdD, MHE, PA-C, Director of Admissions at Georgia Regents University.

9. Dennis Brown, BS, MPH, Clinical Assistant Professor of Physician Assistant Studies, Director of Physician Assistant Program at Quinnipiac University.

10. Alan Platt, PA-c, MMSc, Director of Admissions, Emory Physician Assistant Program.

11. Leah P. Baldwin, Associate Director of Graduate and Professional Programs Admissions, Pacific University.

12. Jamie McDaniel, B.S.M.T., Assistant Professor, Wake Forest School of Medicine

About the Authors

Duke Pasquini, MA Ed

Duke is a retired principal and educator with over 32 years of experience, published author of 3 books, and current state assessor for new teachers and adjunct professor at National University. He has helped many applicants over the course of 3 years perfect their personal statements, a majority who have gone on to be accepted into PA school that very same year. He has written two novels, A Warrior's Son and Teenage Mosaic.

Sue Edmondson

Sue Edmondson has been a freelance writer in Northern Nevada and Northern California since 1999. Her articles have appeared in publications such as Family Pulse, Rlife, Enjoy, Edible Reno-Tahoe and she spent five years as a reporter for the Mountain Echo newspaper. She dabbles in fiction and was awarded first place for short fiction by the Reno News and Review. She's sold several short children's stories. Her other career is as an attorney. After spending seven years practicing family law, she spent the next 19 years at the District Attorney's Office

Stephen Pasquini, PA-C

Stephen is a rural family practice physician assistant since 2004 and creator of www.thepalife.com. He is a National Health Service Corps Scholar and graduate from The University of Medicine and Dentistry of NJ (Rutgers) PA program and the University of Washington in Seattle, WA. Stephen has been working as a mentor and adviser to PA students through his website and personal practice for over 10 years. His passion is helping people express a gift for medicine and healing through the PA profession. His goal is to help compassionate, caring and patient-focused individuals actualize their dream of becoming a physician assistant.

52969379R00051

Made in the USA
San Bernardino, CA
11 September 2019